MW01077404

CHILDREN'S ART

GRobertson '06

ANTJE TESCHE-MENTZEN
HERLINDE KOELBL

CHILDREN'S ART

TEXTS BY
HANS KRIEGER
ANTJE TESCHE-MENTZEN
ERNST PÖPPEL
GERD GRÜNEISL
ALBERT KAPFHAMMER

FREDERKING & THALER

First published as *Kunst von Kindern* in Germany in 2002 by Frederking & Thaler Verlag GmbH, Munich
Infanteriestr. 19, Haus 2, D-80797 Munich
www.frederking-thaler.de

First American edition
Copyright © 2003 Frederking & Thaler Verlag GmbH, Munich

Editor: Kultur & Spielraum e.V., Munich
Text copyright © "I Paint a World of My Own," Antje Tesche-Mentzen, Munich
"Poppies in a Cornfield?" and texts introducing each picture section, Hans Krieger, Munich
"Pictures Conquer Time," Ernst Pöppel, Institute for Medical Psychology, University of Munich
"Children, Creativity, and Art," Gerd Grüneisl and Albert Kapfhammer, Kultur & Spielraum e.V., Munich
The authors have asserted their moral rights to be identified as the authors of the book.
Photographs © Herlinde Koelbl, Munich
Translation © Howard Fine, Munich
The names of the young artists are given in the captions.
Most of the works reproduced here were done on the standard European paper format of 21 x 42 cm.
Copyediting: Daniela Weise, Munich, and Michele Schons, Munich
Design and layout: Monika Neuser, 2005 Werbung, Munich
Production: Büro Caroline Sieveking, Munich
Front cover: Yorck, 4 years old: "Untitled," gouache
Back cover: © Herlinde Koelbl, Munich
Originated by Lorenz & Zeller, Inning a.A.
Printed and bound in Germany by Passavia Druckservice GmbH, Passau

ISBN 3-89405-446-8

All rights reserved under inernational copyright conventions. No part of the book may be reproduced
or utilized in any form or by any means, electronic or mechanical, including photocopying, or by any
information storage or retrieval system, without permission in writing from the publisher.

I PAINT A WORLD OF MY OWN

by Antje Tesche-Mentzen

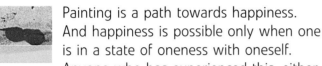 Painting is a path towards happiness. And happiness is possible only when one is in a state of oneness with oneself. Anyone who has experienced this, either consciously as an adult or unconsciously as a child, knows what I mean. In the process of painting or another creative activity, everything else falls away and one experiences a state of weightlessness. Feeling, understanding, and giving shape to experience merge and become a single, unified whole.

Children naturally experience this happiness – if they're allowed to remain free and if one doesn't criticize them or try to influence them. A child's imagination is unlimited. It soars into realms that have long since become inaccessible to us adults. Children link the most incredible things with one another, as though doing so were perfectly natural and logical. There is no "right" and "wrong." Everything is possible. And above all: there's no such thing as "talented" or "untalented." These value judgments are made only in adult life. When children, especially preschool children whom no one has "trimmed" or "instructed," take a brush in hand, it almost seems as though God were painting through them. Their paintings reveal that the inner and outer worlds are indistinguishable.

That's why I begin painting with children as early as possible, often when they are only two years of age. As long as they haven't yet begun to paint figuratively, they develop a very personal sensitivity to colors, and this can offer profound insights into their character. Painting also helps children to overcome their fears and to vent their aggressions. Looking at a child's paintings, one can readily tell how the child feels and what themes occupy his or her mind. A child's choice of forms and colors reflects inner tensions and conflicts.

I've often witnessed the therapeutic efficacy of painting. It helps some children stop stuttering; it helps others to process and thus overcome severe crises in their lives, e.g. the death of a family member. Konstantin's paintings (pp. 88 and 91) are good examples of this. Beginning with his father's death and continuing for the next year, the themes of death and grief continually recur in his paintings. Maximilian (pp. 79 and 86) painted nothing but volcanoes for a long time. He himself was a volcano, and I simply allowed him to be one. Trixi (pp. 74 and 75) lived in India for a year and only later was she able to find images to express the difficult experiences that she had had there. At a very early age I encouraged Christian (pp. 76 and 77) to design his own clothes and to illustrate stories. He's an adult now – and is a well-known costume and stage designer.

A child's sensibilities and emotions flow directly into the paintbrush without first having to overcome the self-doubt, hasty evaluation, and self-criticism that so often inhibit adults. What a pity that these gifts are all too often allowed to languish, unrecognized and unused! It takes so little to make painting possible: a paintbox, a brush, a few large sheets of paper – and the journey begins!

In his later years, Picasso strove to paint like a child. Eighty-year-old painter Karel Appel admits, "I just smear freely." Like a three-year-old? "That's right, but the difference is that I do it." The statement is simple, but it shows how much Appel admires children's spontaneous capacity for self-expression. This means that we should take children's art seriously, that we should appreciate it and preserve it. The years of early childhood are precious: children become "adult" and "reasonable" all too soon. They require sensitive accompaniment, especially when they begin the transition into puberty, a phase during which their capacity for understanding exceeds their technical abilities. Young people's conflicts with themselves and their environment are exposed to a diverse array of influences during this difficult phase. They've lost the spontaneity of early childhood, they compare themselves with role models, and they need to come to terms with their own freedoms.

People who have experienced what it means to become intimate with their own feelings through painting will never want to stop. And, unlike playing a violin, say, the ability to paint doesn't require regular and constant practice.

It doesn't matter whether other people like the picture or are able to understand it. A three-year-old once painted big blue and green arcs across the paper. "I'm painting God," he said. Then he painted a brown bulge. What's that? "God's backpack." "And what does He have inside it?" the other children asked. "Lots of pure love." "No," the little painter said. "Paints and brushes." It's that simple!

Over 30 years of experience at my painting school have taught me to take each child seriously and to respect each individual's uniqueness, regardless of the child's age. I don't expect them to copy me. Children don't need to learn: they need to experience. My own ongoing inquiry into painting and sculpture can help them in this. They see my work–and they hear my doubts.

I offer suggestions and assistance, but I never insist that the child follow my instructions as if he or she were in school. I try to let children find their own paths, and those paths are without a doubt entirely different from my own. I try to spark their enthusiasm for independence, for seeing the world differently and in ways that differ from the way the world is typically described and explained. This applies to all areas of life–not solely to painting.

This book is intended to inspire children and strengthen their desire to paint things that they either cannot or would prefer not to express in words. It's so much easier to keep the natural creativity of early childhood than it is laboriously to regain it later. I hope this book will encourage adults to follow children's example rather than persist in the cowardly belief that expresses itself in phrases like "I can't paint." I hope this book will encourage adults, either alone or together with children, to abandon their inhibitions and leap head over heels into the marvelous adventure of colors and forms.

EVERYTHING IS A MYSTERY

Good morning, star-red. Good morning, lemon-blue. Time has just begun. The horizon is wide open. Everything is without borders, an over-flowing mystery. But there are colors glowing with an inner light. Bubbling and boiling within them is a coming-into-being that doesn't yet know its shape. Or has it left shape and figure behind it long ago? How did things look in God's mind before He created the world?

Julia, 6 years old: "Pattern," acrylic

18

Page 19
Laurenz, 5 years old:
"Untitled," watercolor

Pages 20–21
Tasja, 3 years old: "Red Secret,"
watercolor, felt-tip marker

Pages 22–23
Tasja, 3 years old: "I Want to Write,"
watercolor, felt-tip marker

Tasja · 3 Jahre

ANIMAL DREAMS

Perhaps animals know a little bit more than we know. The spiral snail carries on its colorful back the dream of its snail world. The cat's body stretches all the way to the sun. What does the monkey think when the eye of wisdom is above a brightly colored chain of mountains? We ought to ask the monkey, but how can we ask him if we have grown beyond childhood and already forgotten his language?

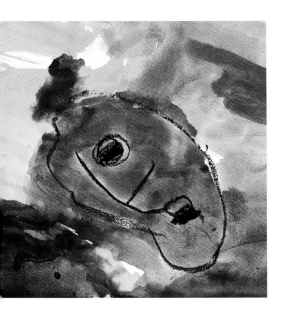

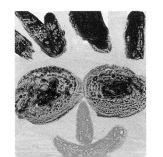

25

Niclas, 4 years old:
"Giraffe," pastel oil-chalk,
watercolor

26

Anette, 7 years old:
"Big Snail with Children,"
pastel oil-chalk, watercolor

Stefanie, 6 years old:
"Cat and Sun,"
oil-chalk, watercolor

29

Stefan, 7 years old:
"Hedgehog, House, and Two Trees,"
pastel oil-chalk, watercolor

Moritz, 5 years old:
"An Enchanted Garden Where Potatoes Grow and a Rock
with a Snake," watercolor

Vivian, 11 years old:
"Tiger in the Jungle,"
oil

Viktoria, 4 years old:
"Cats, and I Too Can Write,"
gouache

Alexandra, 4 years old: "Turtle with Halo," pastels, watercolor

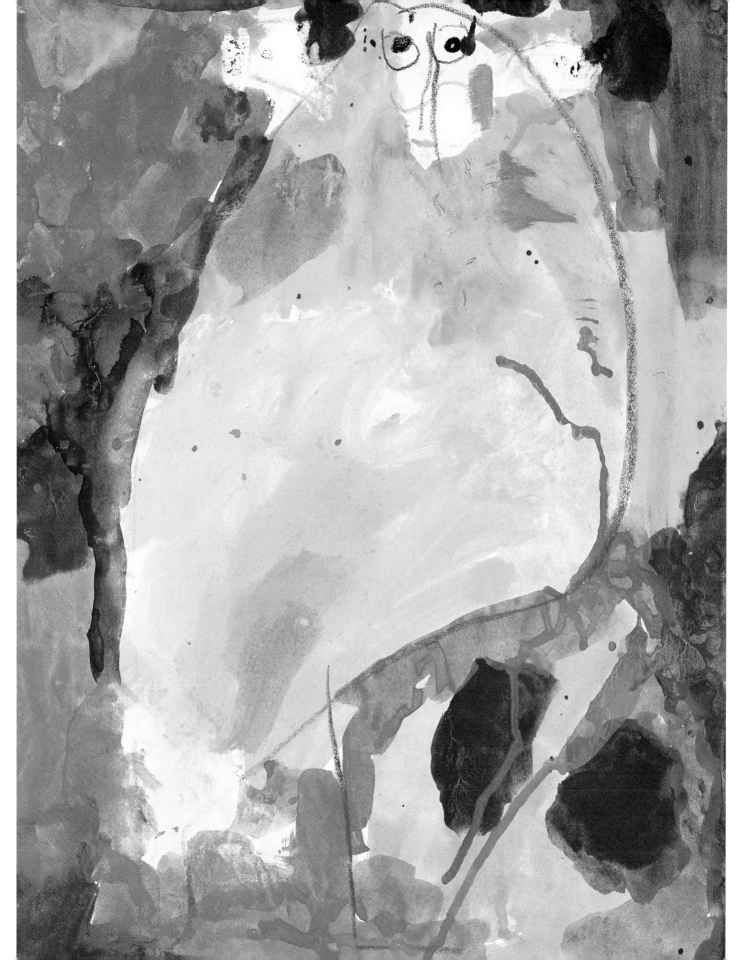

Mona, 3 years old: "Monkey," water-color, chalk

33

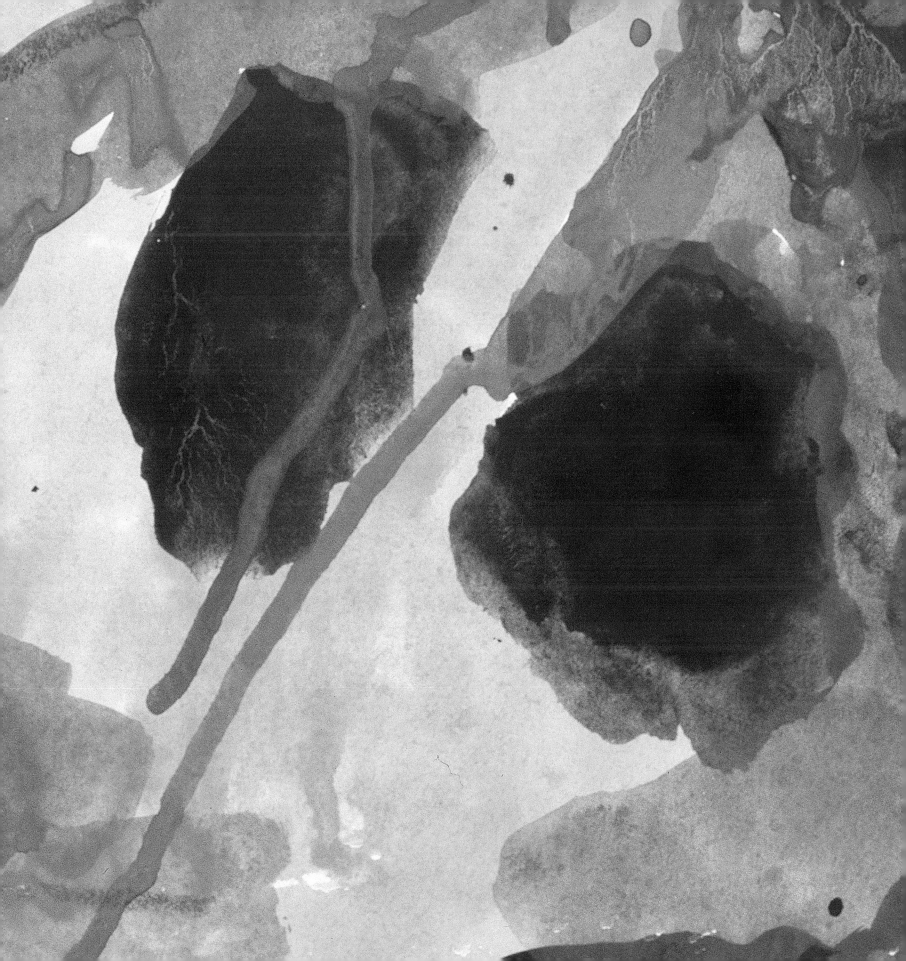

PLANT DREAMS

Flowers are a starry carpet. A finger game from deep water. The foamy crown atop a pale ceramic vessel. Or perhaps an enigmatic eye whose dark pupils will suck you in if you aren't careful. Would they be able to support the sky if the trees didn't already bear the heavens as a golden vault?

37

Julius, 5 years old:
"Fruits with Tree,"
watercolor

Melanie, 5 years old:
"Water Lilies,"
watercolor

Daniel, 5 years old:
"Vase with Yellow
Tulips," watercolor

Pages 42–43
Jan, 14 years old: "In the Garden," detail, watercolor

Pages 44–45
Sophie, 6 years old: "Flowerbed," gouache

Pages 46–47
Leopold, 7 years old: "Poppy Flowers," pastel oil-chalk, watercolor

Solveig, 5 years old:
"Autumn Tree,"
acrylic

ON A JOURNEY

The tower wants to fall, but the blue holds it firmly. How far must one drive to find a miracle when the car is already rolling on wheels made of flowers? Where do pagodas grow? When you're on a journey, you're always outside and inside at the same time.

The ocean is made of stuff that's more real than the ship. And the star is as big and as red as the melting sun.

Page 53
Sebastian, 11 years old:
"Pisa,"
pastel oil-chalk

Page 54
Christian, 6 years old:
"Ship, Red Star, and Glittering Water,"
gouache

Michael, 6 years old:
"Pisa and Paris,"
watercolor and pastel oil-chalk

Penelope, 8 years old: "The Eiffel Tower," watercolor

Jenny, 11 years old:
"Bangkok,"
pastel oil-chalk,
watercolor,
gold Plaka paint

59

Eva, 12 years old:
"By the Sea in
Italy," gouache

60

Mathias, 7 years old:
"City of the Future,"
watercolor

Charlotte, 7 years old:
"A Visit to London:
I, the Queen, With Coach and Royal Guard,"
oil-chalk, gouache

62

Page 63
Mathias, 11 years old: "Through
the Jungle In a Dugout Canoe,"
pastel

Page 64
Jenny, 10 years old:
"New York,"
pastel oil-chalk, watercolor

Julian, 4 years old: "Auto,"
pastel oil-chalk, watercolor

Karoline, 7 years old: "In Traffic,"
chalk and watercolor

FACE TO FACE

 A face is always someone who stands opposite us, even if it's our own. A face is a mysterious continent, with broad expanses where we are likely to lose our way. It's like a blossom on a stalk, a flower whose interior is just coming into view. It has recognizable forms that are never quite the same and that always elude our grasp. A face is fixed by its eyes, as set against a dark background. And how vulnerable it is when it doesn't wear a hat as a mask and protective shield!

Friederike, 8 years old: "Self-portrait," pastel oil-chalk

Page 69
Florian, 7 years old:
"Self-portrait with New
Eyeglasses," pastel oil-
chalk, watercolor

Pages 70–71
Raphaela, 8 years old:
"My Mother and I," pastel
oil-chalk, watercolor

70

Page 72
Annika, 12 years old:
"Portrait of a Beautiful
Woman," oil

Page 73
Hanna, 11 years old:
"My Dream World,
My Hobbies, and I,"
collage, watercolor

Benedict, 8 years old:
"Self-portrait," acrylic

Trixi, 12 years old:
"Indian," oil

74

Trixi, 12 years old:
"Indian," oil

Charlotte, 12 years old:
"Elegant Lady,"
acrylic, pastel oil-chalk

Christian, 10 years old:
"Balinese Person with
Fruits," watercolor

77

FEAR ACCOMPANIES US

Suddenly volcanoes begin to smoke and rumble! Everything is aflame. The charred house must be awfully tiny so that the fear won't be quite so big. Terrors lurk behind a paper-thin wall. Father's death is incomprehensible. Everything becomes bare and barren, as though the colors had died with him. "Never give up" can also mean: paint, paint, and keep on painting until life returns.

80

Page 79
Maximilian, 6 years old:
"Volcanic Eruption,"
watercolor

Page 80
Stefan, 8 years old:
"Minz and Maunz, the Cats,
Raise Their Paws...,"
pastel oil-chalk, watercolor

Page 81
Jörg, 5 years old:
"Beloved Monster,"
acrylic

Konstantin,
12 years old:
"Hope,"
pencil

89

Konstantin, 12 years
old: "Totem," pastel
oil-chalk, gouache

Page 91
Philip, 12 years old:
"Detective Work
in London,"
watercolor

IN THE LAND OF FABLES

Blackness is richly colored in the magical Land of Cockaigne. Labyrinthine paths are there to be walked in the gigantic body of the fabulous animal. Christ's parents stand in a golden halo above the little worm of Jesus. Pegasus and the Three Wise Men are so close beneath the mythic purple. "Who has been eating from my plate?" Even the frightful dragon in front of the paradisaical school can't entirely lose his sense of humor.

Christian, 6 years old: "The Land of Cockaigne," watercolor

Pages 94–95
Nina, 5 years old:
"Hänsel and Gretel,"
pastel oil-chalk, watercolor

Pages 96–97
Marc, 10 years old:
"Warrior's Tomb," pastel oil-chalk
and Plaka paint on colored paper

95

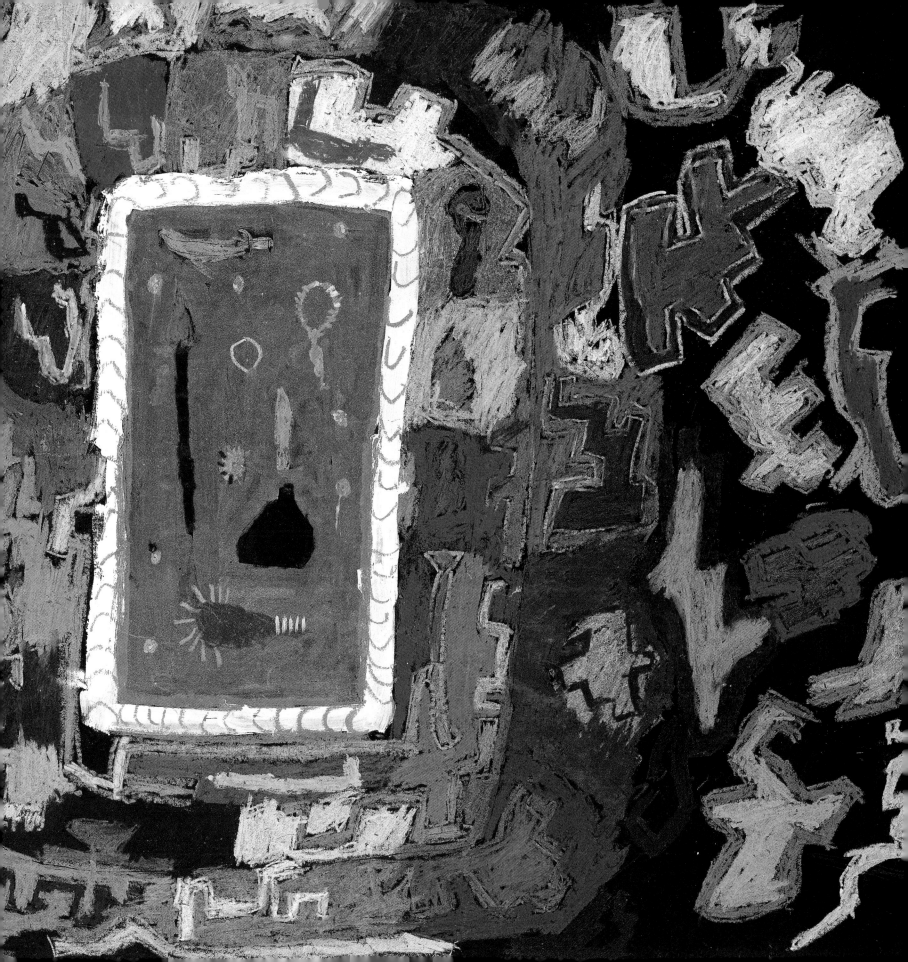

Harriett, 4 years old:
"Princess and Seven Dwarfs,"
watercolor

98

Page 99
Hanna, 6 years old:
"Pegasus, Princess with Secret
and Flower," pastel oil-chalk

Pages 100–1
Maximilian, 5 years old:
"Mary and Joseph with the Christ Child and Colorful
Houses," pastel oil-chalk, watercolor

Page 102
Leopold, 7 years old:
"The God of Thunder,"
pastel oil-chalk, watercolor

Page 103
Tassilo, 12 years old:
"Labyrinth through a Beast,"
felt-tip marker, watercolor

Pages 104–5
Katrin, 10 years old:
"Dragon-Fright Labyrinth,"
felt-tip marker, watercolor

MASKED PLAY AND PUPPET DANCE

The oriental princess awakens beneath the tower's onion-shaped dome and shakes her magical cloak. Puppets dance on the stage where the masked play is performed. The double-bass is there too with its bulging airy belly. Snowmen laugh about the rumor which insists that they must be white.

Susanne,
12 years old:
"One Dances
Wildly at Carnival
Time," felt-tip
marker

107

Julia, 4 years old:
"Carnival Princess,"
gouache

108

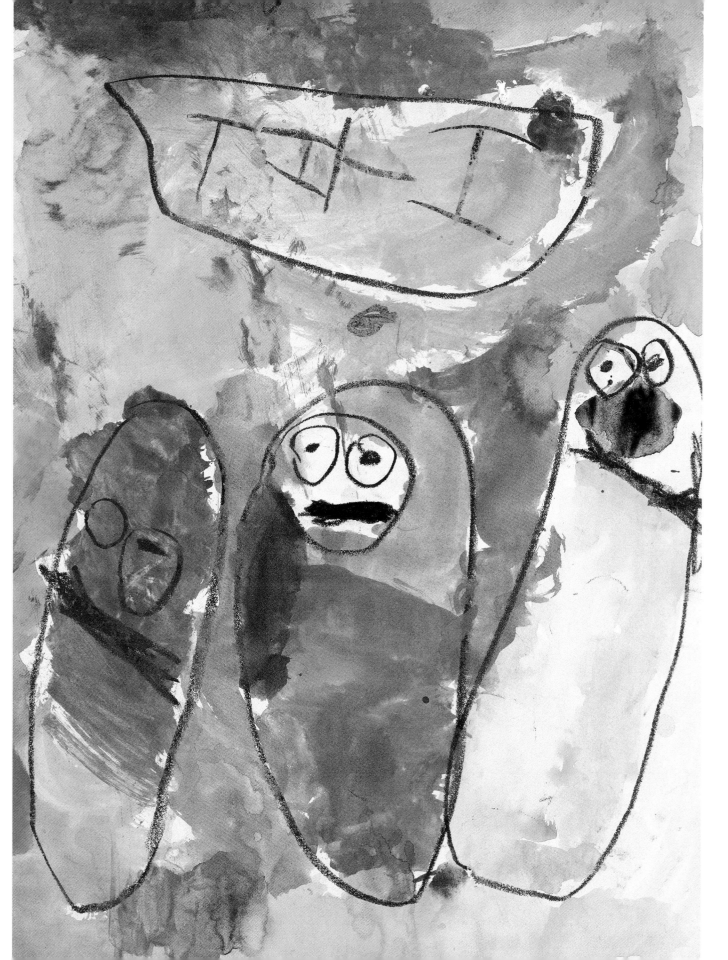

Alexandra, 3 years old:
"My Dolls and T. and H.,
as My Grandpa and
Grandma Are Named,"
watercolor, chalk

109

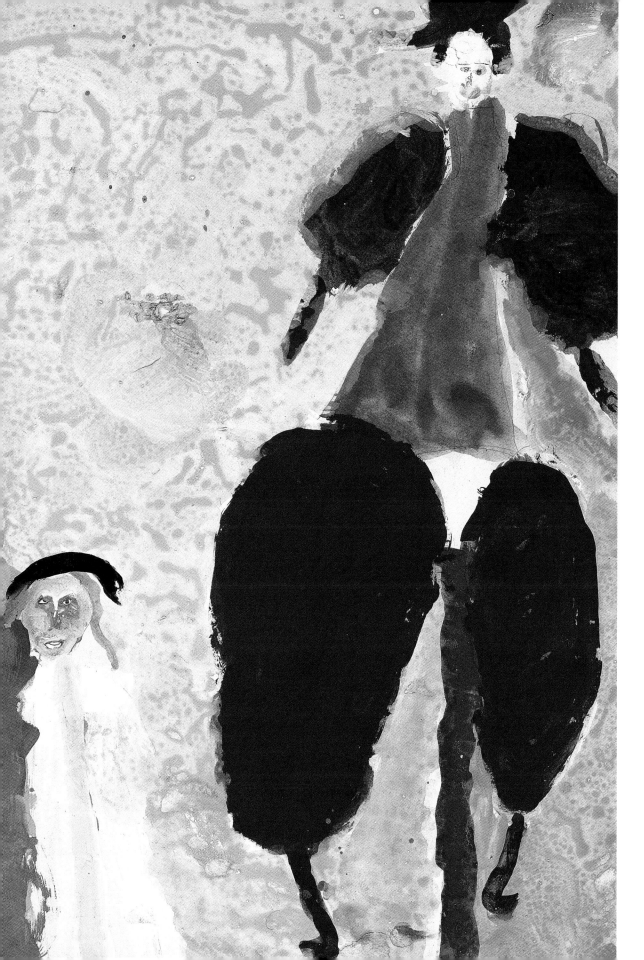

Stefan, 9 years old:
"Cello and Old Dolls,"
acrylic

Jessica, 8 years old:
"Marionette and Snowman Made of Candy,"
watercolor, pastel oil-chalk

Felix,
7 years old:
"Mask,"
acrylic

Markus,
8 years old:
"Mask,"
acrylic

ON THE THRESHOLD

Who can still remember when and how he or she stepped out of childhood? There was no gate to open, no distinct threshold to cross. Everything changed gradually and unnoticeably. The choice of line becomes more decisive, more willful. The planned and the practiced begins to reshape and cover the spontaneous. Role models are transformed or consciously covered up. Sometimes a person is lucky: he or she is able to rescue the imagination and carry it over into adult life. Such people are described as "gifted." But who gives this gift? And what about all the others who had plenty of imagination when they were still wholly children?

Page 121, left
Hexi, 10 years old:
"After Nude Sketching,"
watercolor, acrylic

Page 121, right
Hexi, 14 years old:
"I Hate You...,"
pastel oil-chalk

Mathias, 16 years old:
"Haunted House and
Chess Knight,"
oil

Barbara, 16 years old:
"After September 11th,"
oil

123

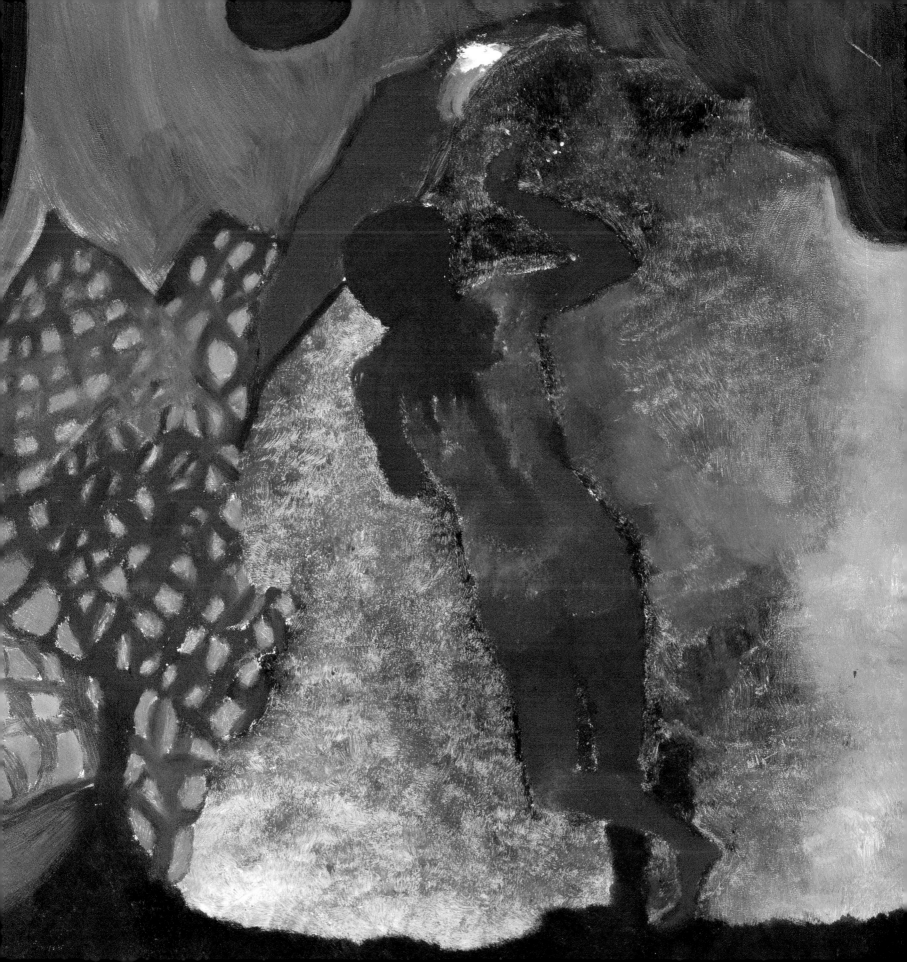

POPPIES IN A CORNFIELD?

What We Can Learn from Children's Art

by Hans Krieger

 The world is a work of the imagination. We were only unconsciously woven into reality. The sole intimations that we would have of reality would be the compulsions in which it entangles us—were it not for the fact that we can maintain a sense for the possible which gives us the freedom that comes from keeping our distance. It is this freedom of distance that creates the open horizon in front of which blind reality can become an actual world. This real world addresses us and involves us. It's much more than merely a programmed pattern of stimulus mechanisms in which we have been functionally adapted like a gear on its axis.

This distance arises when thing and idea separate from one another. The imagined thing is not the real thing, yet paradoxically participates in it. The thing is simultaneously present and absent in our imagination: present in the imagination, yet never entirely identical with it. This creates a difference, and along with this difference comes the possibility of being different. Thanks to the possibility of being different, the being of things gains the openness of mystery and thus first acquires the clearer contours of its presence for people: as a network knit not of facts, but of relationships. What we call "world" is not the sum of "all that is real," but the sum of all the possibilities of relationship that can potentially be experienced.

Relationship arises through identity in the non-identical, i.e. through symbolic linkage. Its basic figures are word and image. Both are equally primordial. In word as well as in image, something takes the place of a thing, something that simultaneously is and is not that thing. And it is in this difference that worlds are engendered through relationships that confer meaning. In other words: through imagination.

Idea and image and reciprocal conditions. The power of the imagination is the precondition for the ability to give shape, and this imaginative power yearns to become concrete in the form of an image through which it can evolve towards clarity. Drawing, painting, and sculpting are basic forms of this elucidating work on the idea of the world. Without this work, no world would be possible for humans. In the pictorial artwork, the idea coalesces into a visible figure and thus becomes part of the sensually perceptible reality that we acquire for ourselves through the power of the imagination. Each picture is therefore not so much a representation of the world, but embodies instead another small step in the endless human process of bringing forth and transforming the world.

A time when humans were already wholly human but hadn't yet created any pictures and hadn't yet responded to the visibility of creation by themselves creating symbolically figurative signs is as inconceivable as a time when humans hadn't yet acquired language. Humankind didn't bring forth speech and visual art: speech and images brought forth humankind. We'll probably never know when the first group of hunters began to use spoken sounds to communicate and cooperate, nor will we ever know who first scratched the silhouette of a bison in a sandy patch of soil or onto the wall of a Paleolithic cave. But only after these actions occurred can we be sure that we're dealing with *Homo sapiens.* The philosopher Hans Jonas convincingly showed that the toolmaking intelligence of *Homo faber* and the visualizing power and imagistic capacity, i.e. the imaginative power, of *Homo pictor* (the painting and drawing human) are reciprocally conditional rather than mutually independent.

The existence of pictorial representations has become such an integral part of our environment that we are only rarely able to be astonished by it. And yet its sheer existence is the greatest of all miracles. All it takes are a few strokes with a pencil or a few patches of paint on a sheet of paper or other background and the beginnings of something that is equivalent to a world appear before our eyes. This new world obviously differs from the one that we think we already know, but it is also intimately interwoven with it. The new world communicates with the old one and intervenes in it. Whenever we see a sketch or a painting, we have the chance to experience a reminder of how we once were, who we are now, and how that which we call "the world" first came into existence for us.

If a child is still child enough and hasn't allowed some adult to exile him or her from the spontaneity and uninhibited freedom of the search for creation, then he or she experiences the full immediacy of the miracle of becoming human and engendering a world when drawing or painting. There are probably few or no children who don't feel the urge to use drawing and painting to "express" themselves, i.e. to carry inner experience into the visible realm of the outside world. As long as the widespread misunderstanding persists that figurative, "true to life" representation is an essential task for art, the pictorial creations of children will continue to be regarded as clumsy, unskilled, touchingly inept, and worthy of our considerate condescension. In the meantime, however, we've learned to see differently, to recognize in children's art a repetition of that primal moment of self-discovery and world-discovery from which all human culture emerges and through which it must continually renew itself.

Of course, neuronal maturation, differentiation and refinement of motor skills, and perceptive abilities also occur when children paint. But the decisive factor is the openness of the act of drawing, which also involves drawing something out of oneself. Rather than attempting to imitate given models, the act of drawing or painting knits anew the fabric of relationship to the world that always appears to us as an external reality, but that is simultaneously also inextricably interwoven with the invisible threads of our inner life. An obsolete yet classical definition of art is the "imitation of nature." In the meantime, we've realized that rather than imitating what has already been created, art echoes the process of natural creation itself.

The magic that we feel in children's paintings has nothing to do with the nostalgia of the as yet unskilled. Children's art, in which nothing must bear verisimilitude to a reality that we adults think we know, reminds us of the early flash of opening, the moment when reality first emerged from the womb of possibility, when the pattern of the world hadn't yet become reified into the illusion of finality. Children's art can teach us that reality is a work of the imagination.

Fantasy and imagination can be disturbing because they don't respect the fence that we've erected to contain the fields of utilitarian practicality and the plots of ownership in a notion of the world that has hardened into familiarity and habit. But imagination is the essentially lively element in the human spirit–and we desperately need its vitality. Imagination is the subject of much talk and much attention in our educational institutions, but the imagination is seldom truly welcomed and cultivated there. Imagination is treated like a poppy in a cornfield: it's lovely to look at, but nonetheless a weed with little or no practical value. At best, the imaginative act of painting and drawing (like making music) is regarded as a pretty but inessential addition, a noble luxury for a recreational break from the earnestness of "real" life or for the few minutes of relaxation after the "real" work has been done.

We ought to know better. Without being rooted in the sense of possibility that aesthetics provide, without the unfocused, roaming opening of the imaginative ability, and without the emotional motivation of artistic expression, the human spirit would be sterile and thus incapable of coping with today's tasks and tomorrow's challenges. The entire educational venture stands and falls along with the lessons known in schools as "art and music." Not even the sheer communication of factual knowledge can function without instruction in art and music, because genuine knowledge presupposes the processing of information by the entire person. What sense would the academic notion of "achievement" make if it didn't include the accuracy of perception, the refinement of psychomotorics and social sensibility, the noncompulsory exploration of possibilities, discipline in the pursuit of a goal that is experienced as meaningful, and the link between acquired competencies and responsibility for one's own actions? To speak in images rather than words: There can be no cornfield without poppies.

As long as educational policy fails to grasp this equation, i.e. as along as it remains as backward as it currently is, hope can rest only in private initiatives such as the "schools of the imagination" that Rudolf Seitz founded and schools of painting like the one run by Antje Tesche-Mentzen, from whose educational work the pictures collected in this volume grew.

PICTURES CONQUER TIME

by Ernst Pöppel

When I look at children's pictures, I feel wonder and sadness. I'm delighted by the immense energy of expression that slumbers within us. And I'm saddened that this energy becomes buried. A friendly turtle smiles at me; I experience the eruption of a volcano; delicate floral patterns grow in yellow hues; sexual fantasies dominate a mind; a cat gazes at me thoughtfully; I'm transported into the future or carried off to Bangkok.

Children's pictures prompt me to ask myself why we draw and paint in the first place, why we seek to put something into a picture. Naturally, as a researcher who studies seeing, I know what everyone else knows (because this knowledge is the most natural thing in the world): namely, that my awareness is an awareness of images. Only in a state of deep sleep am I wholly without images. Images dominate waking and dreaming consciousness. I see something in every instant: colors, planes, outlines that form themselves into objects or living beings like the tree in front of me, the face that smiles at me, the script that's left behind when my hand propels my pen.

I share this omnipresence of images with all animals that have the sense of sight. Through my eyes, I construct an image of the world for myself. My worldview takes shape. One thing that's shared by all sighted living creatures is that these images exist in the present moment. Each image that appears before my eyes is always here and now. Even an image in a dream is a contemporary

image. Only after I have awakened do I sense that a doubling of world occurred when the dreamed image appeared. In my dream, I saw scenes and encountered people whose images had been stored within me, even if these images were sometimes distorted. The dreamed image thus teaches me that the image that I have in my waking consciousness at this moment may not be lost forever because it can reappear in a dream. This may not necessarily be true for every image in waking life, but it surely applies to the images associated with experiences that touch me powerfully.

We share the theater of dreams with many other animals. But after humans and animals awaken, they pursue different paths. Only humans draw, paint, sculpt, give shape, and thus create socially visible images from their internal images. An urge towards structure is apparent in this process of designing. Rather than merely distributing pigments and covering surfaces, when a human being paints or draws he or she always designs something. As we can see in this book, the urge towards figurative depiction already exists in early childhood. Young children produce pictures of humans and animals; they draw geometrical objects; and they do all this with a delicate aesthetic. We recall, of course, that the essential meaning of the Greek word *aisthesis* is "perception."

Why do human beings seek to capture something in a picture? What is their underlying motivation? We make (ourselves) an image in order to overcome the fleetingness of the moment and to conquer the transience of time. In a picture, we can capture an instant and preserve it forever. A picture "freezes" something from the past so that we can "defrost" it later on. In a picture, we invent our past and recognize our future. By creating a picture, we step out of momentary experience. Indeed, not until we draw a picture do we determine ourselves as human beings–because two essential conditions of our existence are an orientation into the future and a sense of being rooted in the past. Only in a temporal anchoring that transcends the fetters of the present can we exist together with others.

This power to create images is inherent in us all, but do we live in accord with it? Modern brain research has shown that our natural potentials, including the ability to create images, do not take effect unless they are imprinted during the early phases of our lives. We enter the world equipped with an excess supply of connections between nerve cells. Imprinting means that the potential with which nature has provided us in the form of predisposition is confirmed through active experience. Potentials that are not confirmed and not used are finally "switched off" and cannot be re-awakened. This applies to our perceptions, feelings, and memories, and it also applies to our volition. The entire repertory of lived experience and conscious representation is shaped by the confirmation it receives through learning. Of course, it is also true that only partial sets of potential experiences are imprinted, although this imprinting doesn't become explicit. This can serve as a starting point for subsequent learning, although the later timeframe of this learning makes it more difficult. Part of being human is being able to create a framework within, which we can unfurl ourselves in accord with our inherent potentials. And fortunate indeed is the person who succeeds in doing so.

CHILDREN, CREATIVITY, AND ART

by Gerd Grüneisl and Albert Kapfhammer, Kultur & Spielraum e.V.

 Children and art: behind this pair of concepts stand many years of inquiry into two questions. Is it valid to link these two concepts in the first place? And to what degree can children become the creators of artworks? These questions were first given serious consideration towards the end of the 19th century, when Corrado Ricci declared that the childish graffiti on the arcades of Bologna deserved to be classified as works of art. Ricci's attention had been schooled through his studies of art history, so the expressive images born from childish fantasies did not escape his notice and he was able to recognize them for what they were: visual testimony to sorrows, joys, and daily experiences.

At about the same time, Europeans discovered the works of non-European artists. These artworks had long been unashamedly devalued and relegated to the genre of "primitive art" because European aesthetic standards had been formulated by men who were indoctrinated with a colonialist notion of cultural hegemony. Naive art, too, its most obvious exponent, customs officer Henri Rousseau, experienced unprecedented recognition. Above all the artists themselves found their way, through paintings and sculptures, to more original forms of expression that were far removed from of what the academic art world courted as "auratic" art. Consequently, artists such as Paul Klee, Jean Dubuffet, and Pablo Picasso occupied themselves with the world of children's pictures and were inspired to create a language of forms and a palette of colors from the trove of treasures embodied in children's art.

After artists made the initial discovery of the richness of design possibilities inherent in children's pictures, people who had been trained in the academic discipline of art history transformed this discovery into a program. Finally, teachers of art (especially the ones who were active in art academies) banished art from this program, as though art had sought a liaison with education. The monopolization of art without respecting the conditions under which art becomes possible led to a trivialization of art education (such as art lessons), robbing it of the impulses it might have been able to offer fledgling artists.

A primary objective of artistic expression is to "disturb" people's ordinary, everyday perception, to heighten people's awareness of the unexpected and the strange, both within and without, and to it prompt people to discover the possibility of another world beyond the realm of concrete, material reality. Artists dared to venture into this unexplored terrain, even if its exploration entailed the risks of being misunderstood or not understood at all and of producing artworks that were despised rather than appreciated. Countless examples of this can be found in the history of art. In his celebrated *History of Art* (1996), art historian Ernst H. Gombrich writes: "The general public lives with the belief that an artist is there to make art, just as a shoemaker is there to make shoes. For most people, this means that an artist ought to create the sort of paintings or sculptures which have already been certified as 'art' in the past. One can understand this vague desire, but unfortunately this is the only service that a true artist cannot render."

Children are treated much the same way artists are, although the recognition that the two groups are treated similarly shouldn't be construed to mean that they can be equated with one another. Doing so would do a disservice to both the children and the artists. Children perceive and think differently because they have only just begun to experience schooling under a pedagogic rationality that deprives them of their unprejudiced viewpoint and uninhibited hand. Precisely this unbiased gaze and this free hand are what enable children to see and interpret the world differently, to be curious about the manifold phenomena and relationships that populate the world. The many efforts intended to help children exercise their right to their own cultural forms of expression are nullified and obliterated by a style of education that filters everything through its own notion of what constitutes learning: namely, one that insists that the only things that are academically valid are those which can be taught, monitored, and given a grade from A to F. This, of course, patently contradicts the spirit of artistic creativity.

"Show me your wounds" would be an appropriate title for this chapter in the history of art and art education. Let us not forget that art doesn't need education, but education needs art! It needs art in the form of aesthetic education, which trains perception to become aware not only of that which lies close at hand, but also to appreciate all the cultural and social phenomena that enrich the world we live in. Education needs to learn from art that there are infinitely many forms of expression, that these expressive forms make possible self-determination and a fertile impetus for learning and experiential activity, that they convey sensuality, and that, above all, they create the freedom to concern oneself with the truths of the world. "If there were only one truth," Pablo Picasso said, "one couldn't paint 100 pictures on the same theme."

Therefore, aesthetic education must necessarily seek new and different locations for learning, venues that can keep the promise that is implicit in working with artistic form-giving. More than just one possibility exists to accomplish this. Many different sites offer themselves as potential locations where children can experience and explore the possibilities of art, where they can be given the necessary time, space, materials, and tools.

Viewed in this light, it becomes apparent that aesthetic education has several tasks to fulfill. First of all, it should make it clear to children that they are allowed to be different, that they have the right to be chaotic, wild, and anarchic, and that they are free to create and give orders of their own in a world in which adults have not yet succeeded in establishing global order. A second task for aesthetic education is to create a transitional zone between art and daily life, i.e. between art and "non-art." Without this zone, there can be neither communication nor evolution of a creativity aimed at coping with life. Thirdly, aesthetic education should strive to ensure that children acquire competencies that are not restricted solely to drawing and painting, but that enable children to communicate and collaborate with others in the pursuit of projects whose goal it is to create a humane future that will be worth living in.

It is understandable that these goals cannot readily be achieved solely with paper, paintbrushes, and paintboxes because an aesthetic education of this sort needs milieus of its own that create a public for the children, that stimulate them to occupy themselves with one another and the world around them so that their activities can develop into cultural forms of living. This succeeds only in social situations that neither isolate the children's creative process nor trivialize its products. This can be guaranteed only when the children's form-giving work occurs under the genuine conditions of artistic production, i.e. in the atmosphere of an atelier or workshop, with access to artists' tools and techniques, and above all with artists' special ways of perceiving the things that can be given shape.

Diverse possibilities exist for creating correspondingly favorable milieus for children. A decisive factor is that children and artists, materials, tools, and media all be brought together so that the children can explore and experience creative form-giving in the artistic process. We hope that this book will stimulate and encourage many people, in many places and for many years to come, to accept the challenges of this important cultural and art-educational work with children.

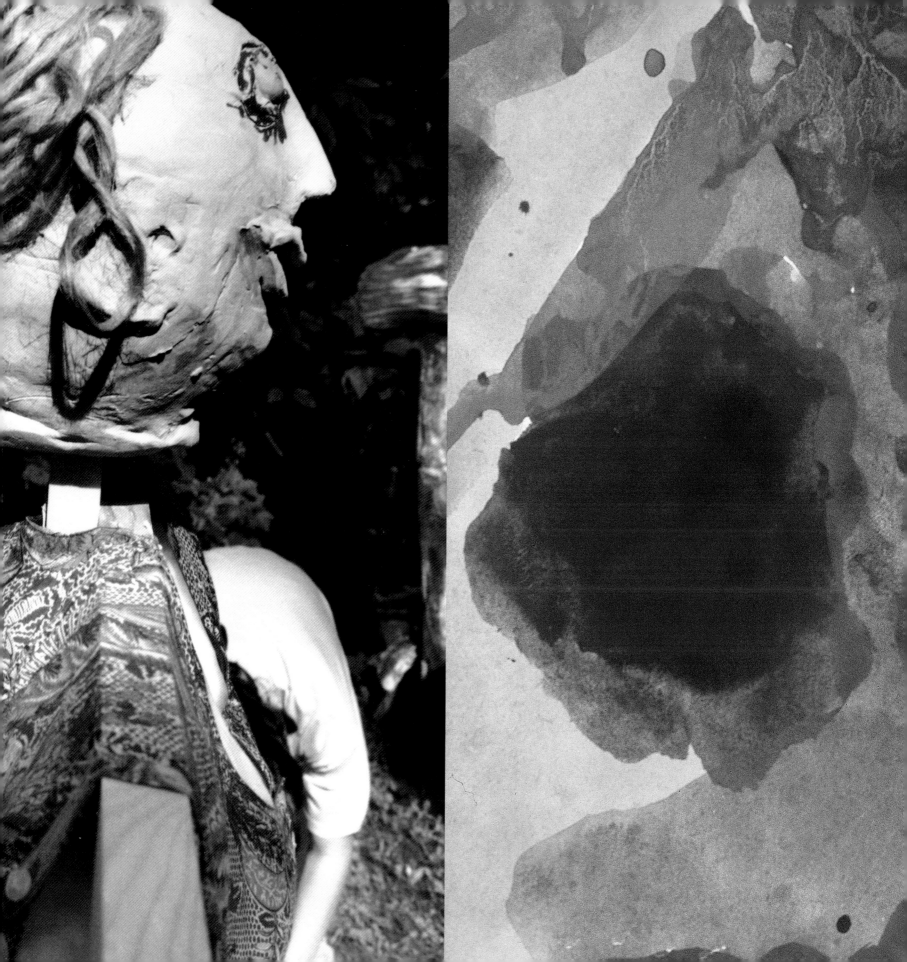